Paul Gauguin … !

Alexander Cloudoncolorsky

DEDICATION

In memory of Paul Gauguin.

CONTENTS

ACKNOWLEDGMENTS

To Painting of Paul Gauguin.

1 CHAPTER
PAUL GAUGUIN … !

Painting of 21 century is a pupil of great painters.

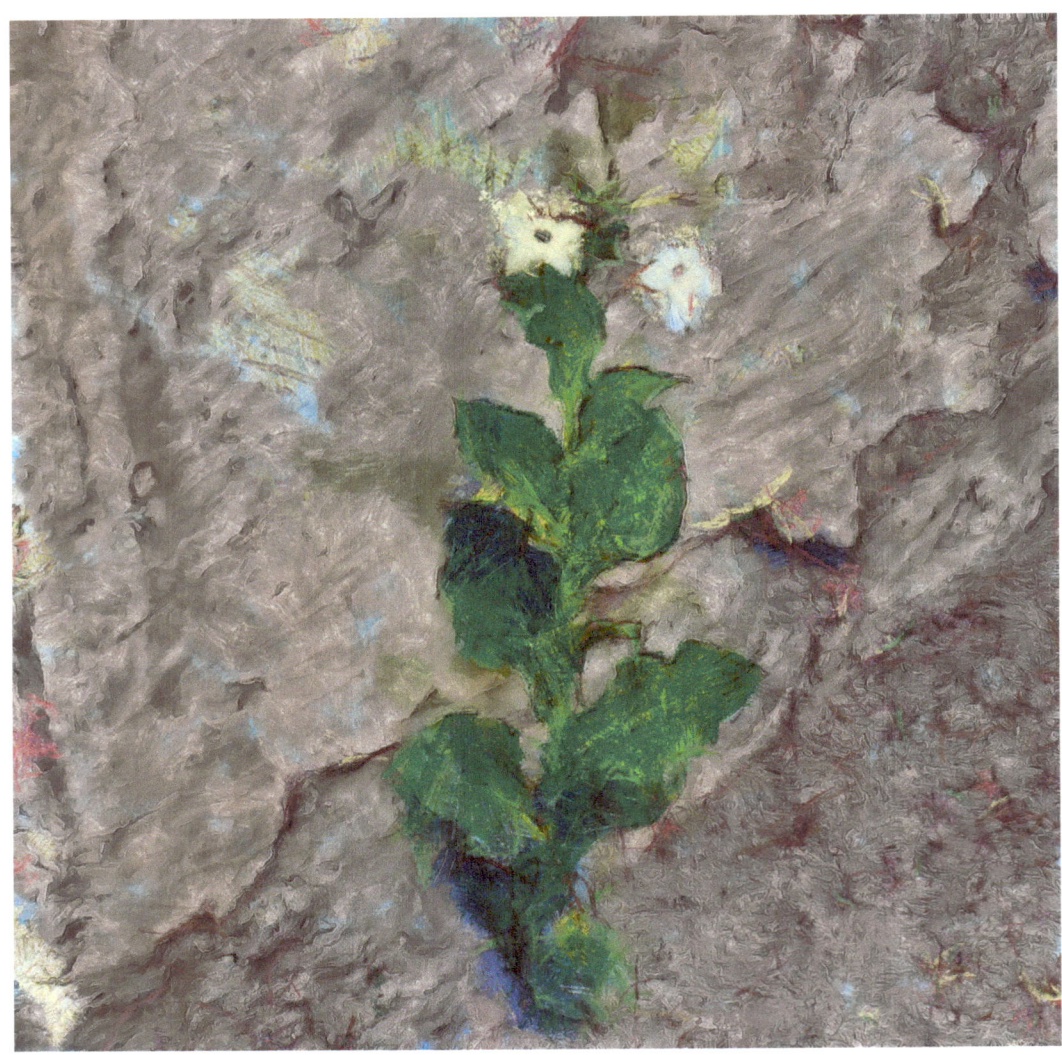

Paul Gauguin … !

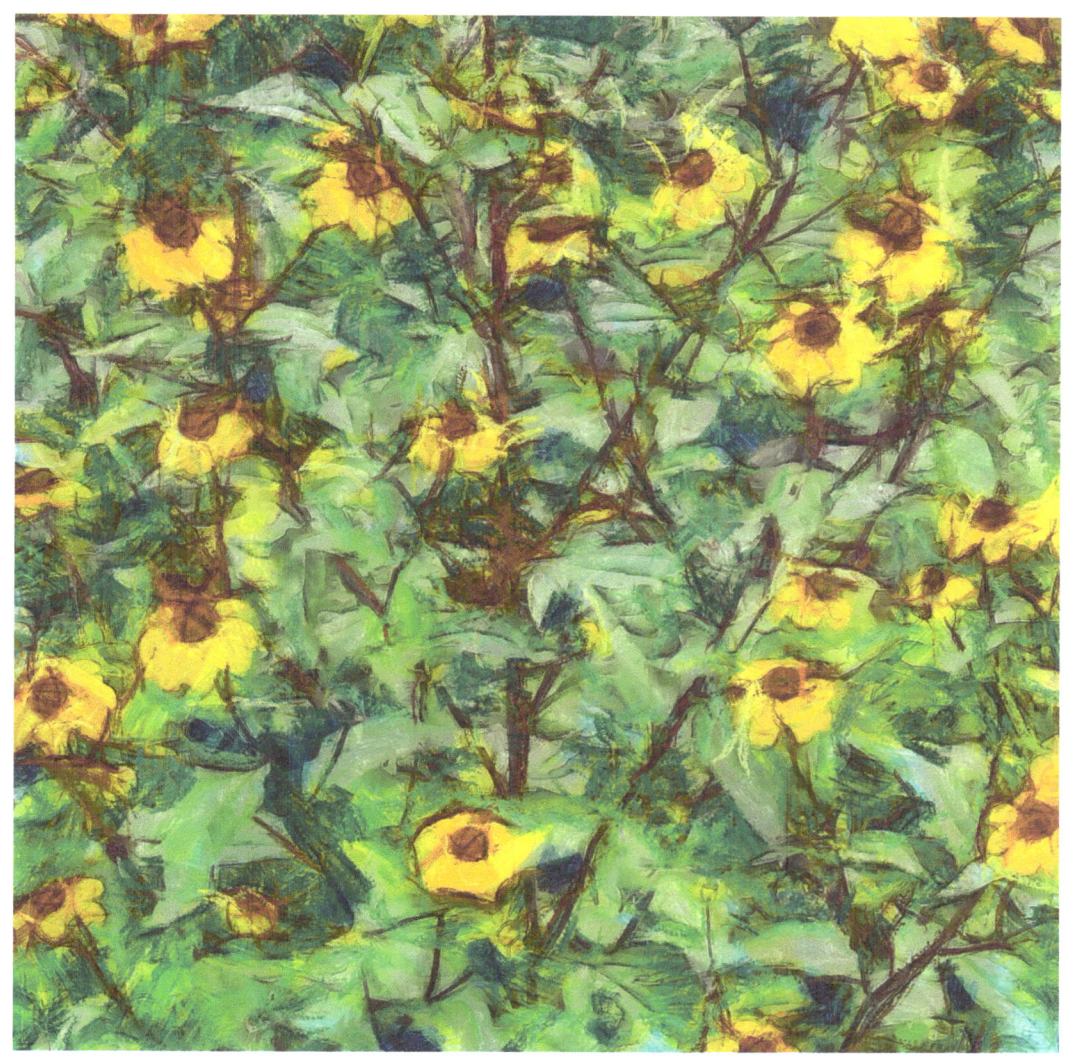

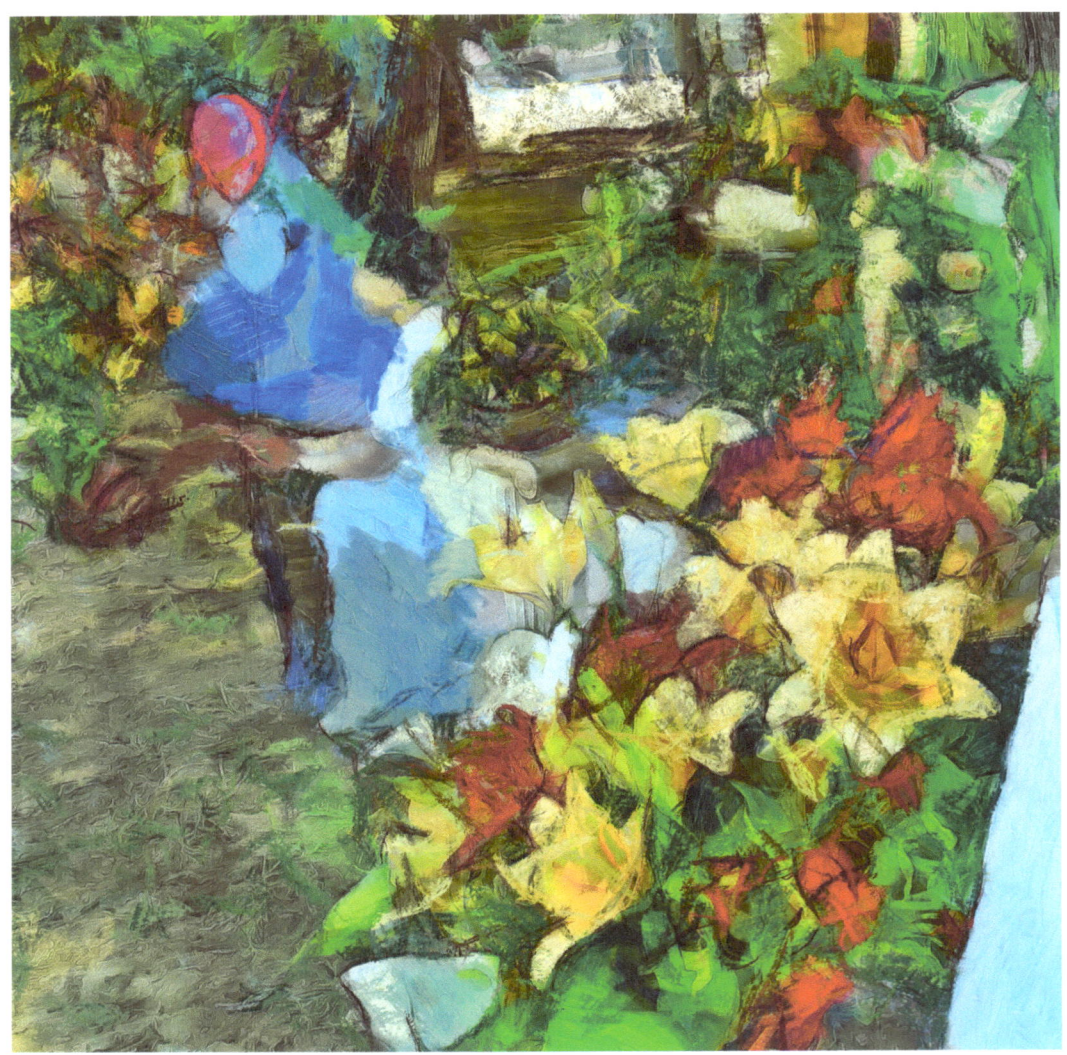

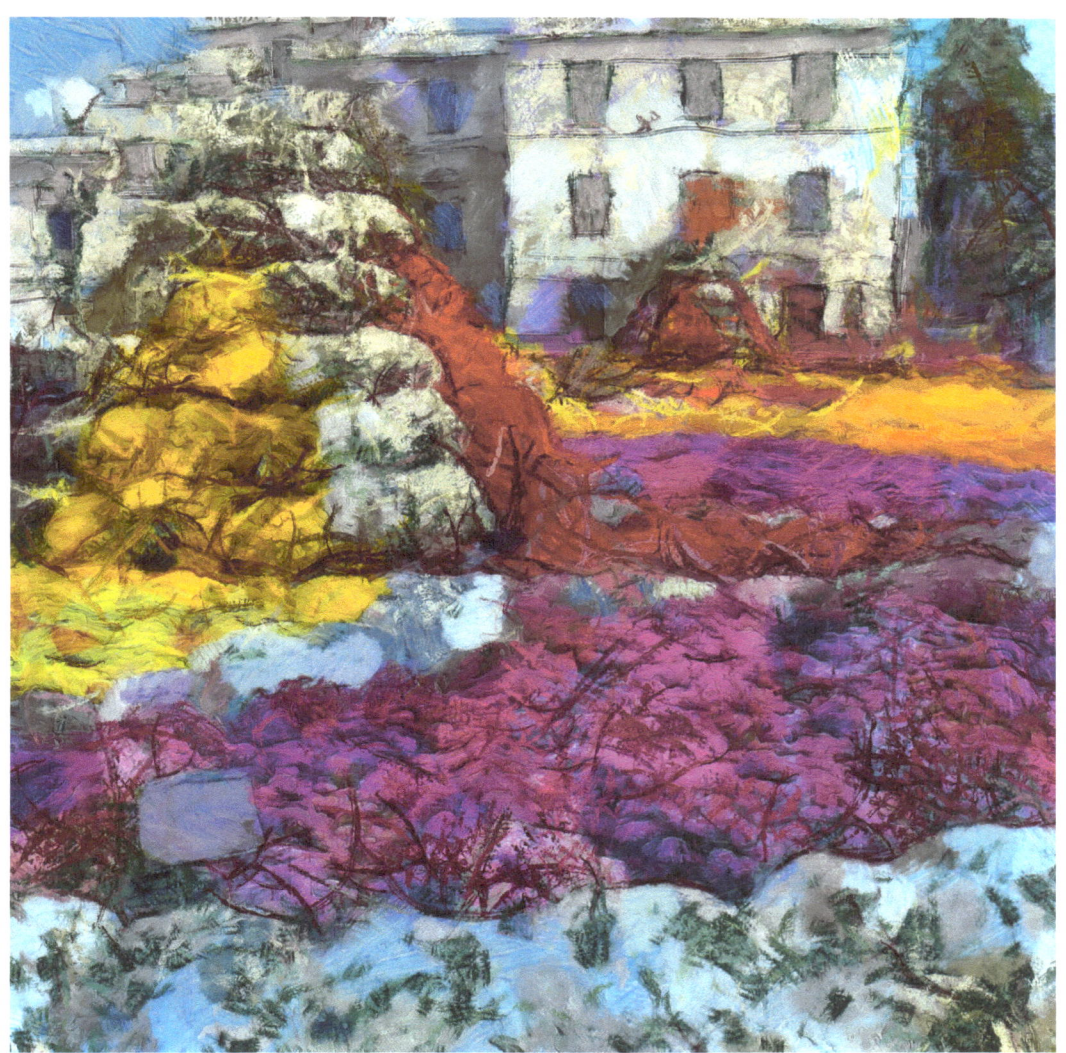

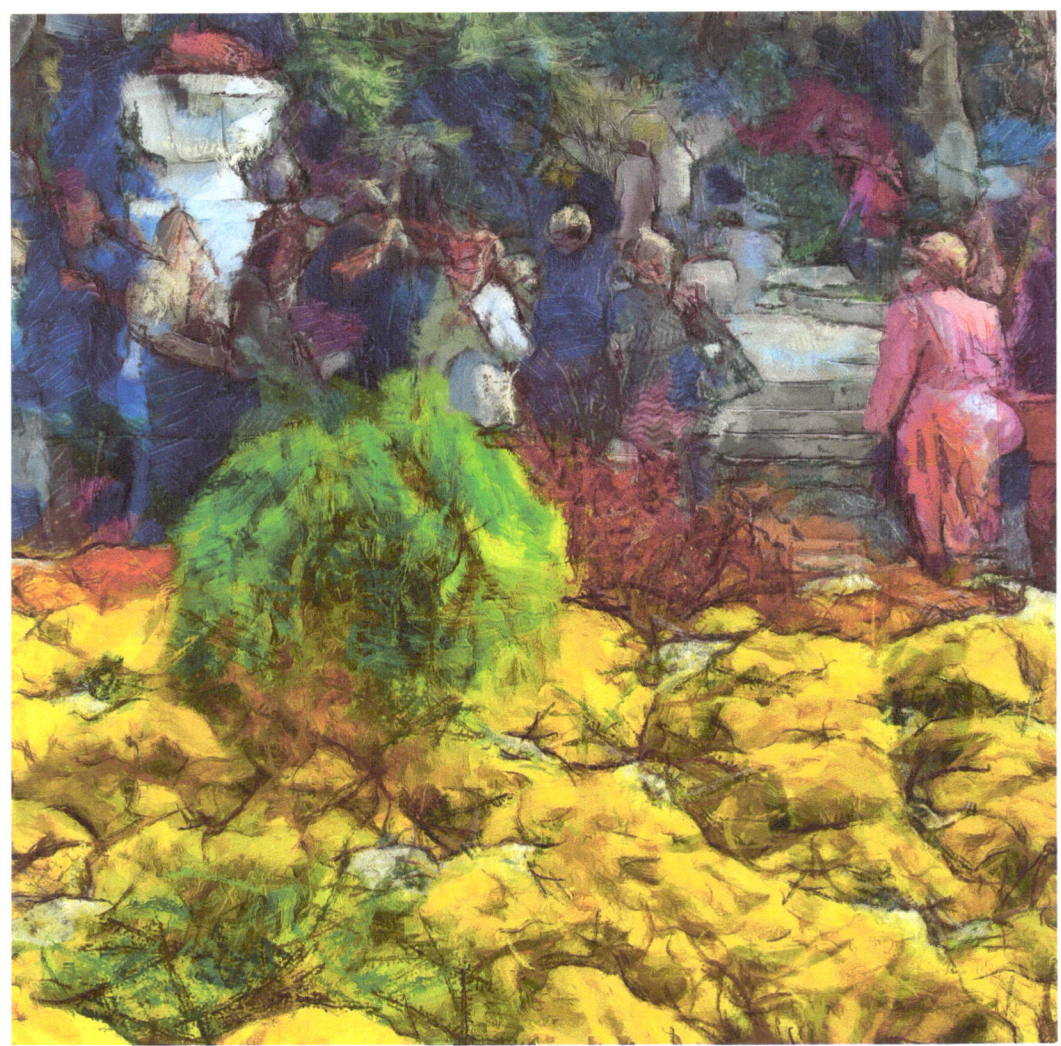

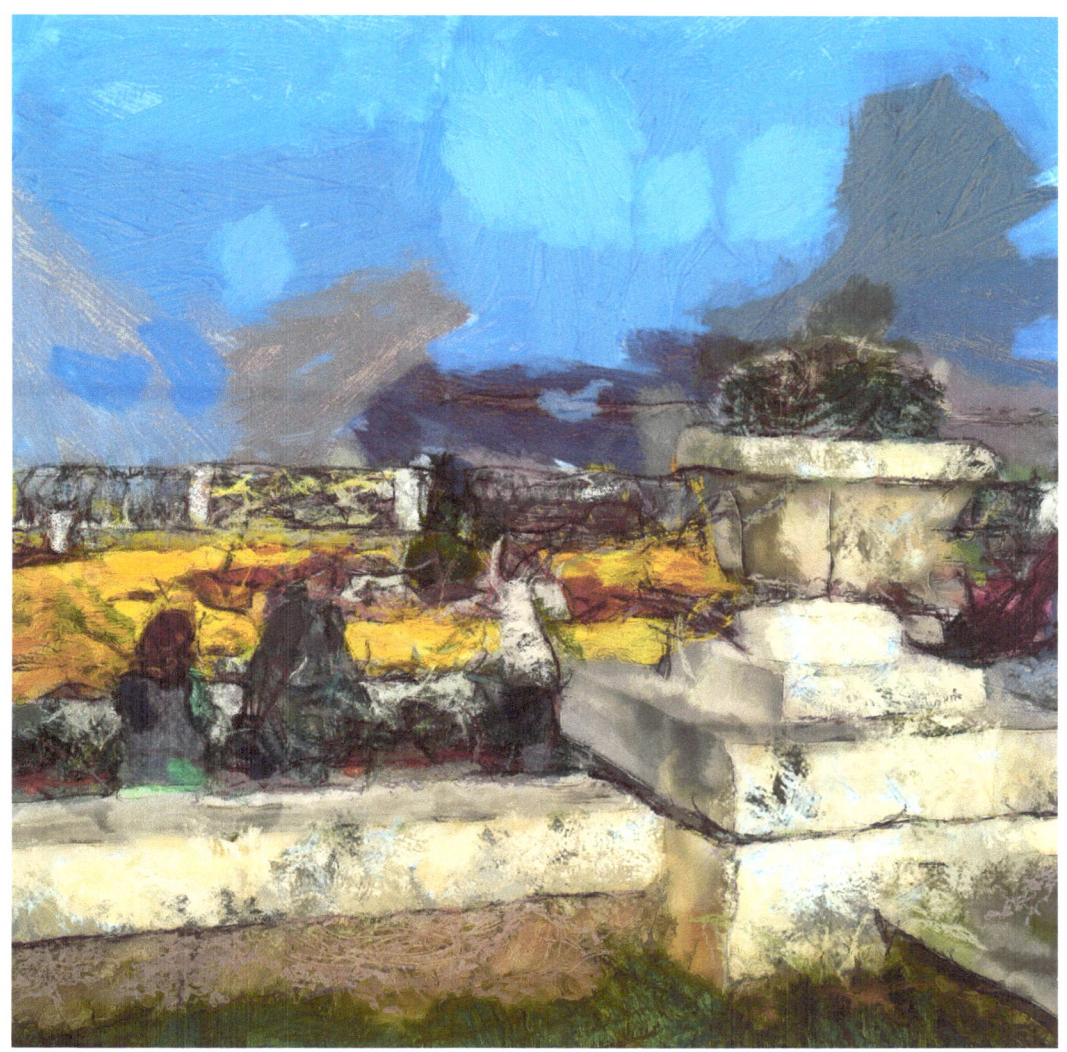

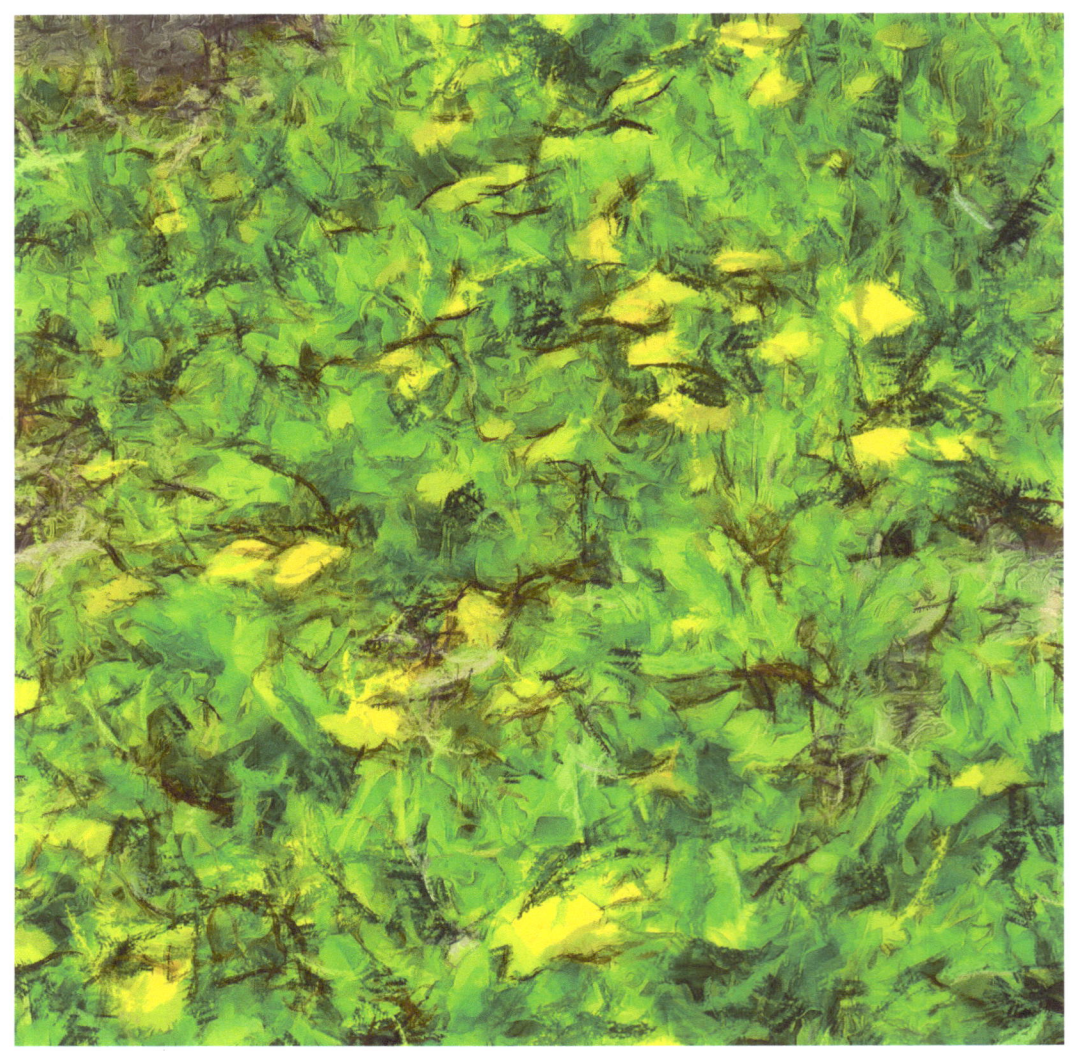

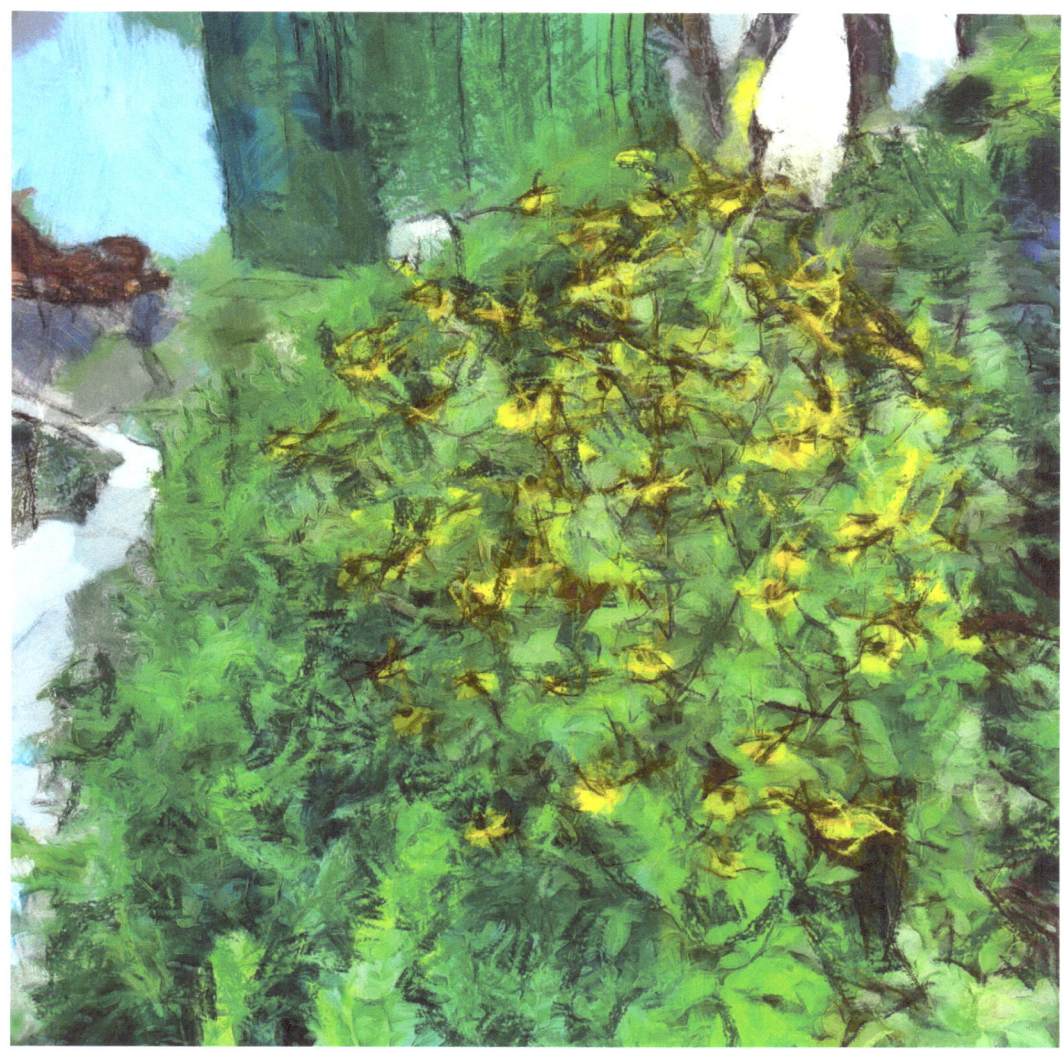

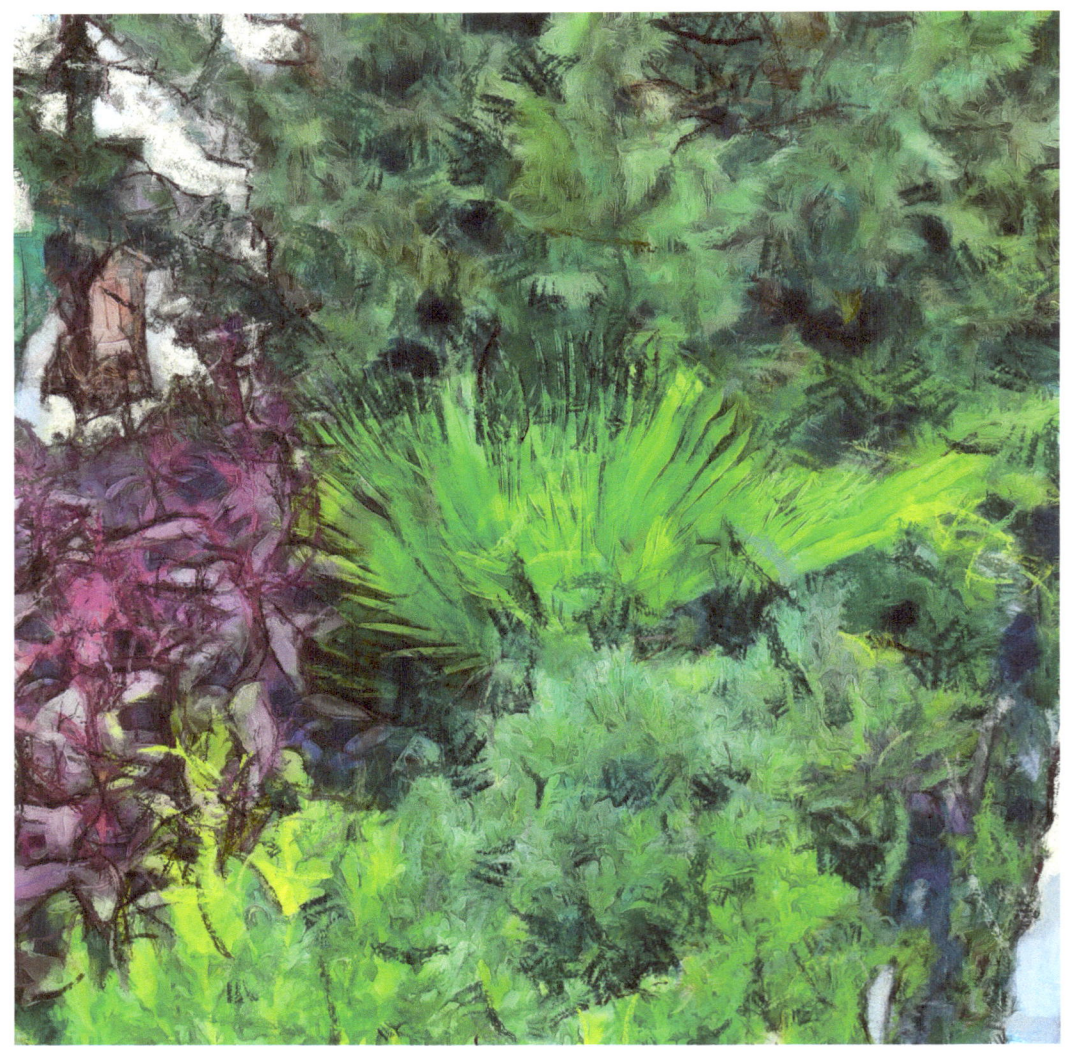

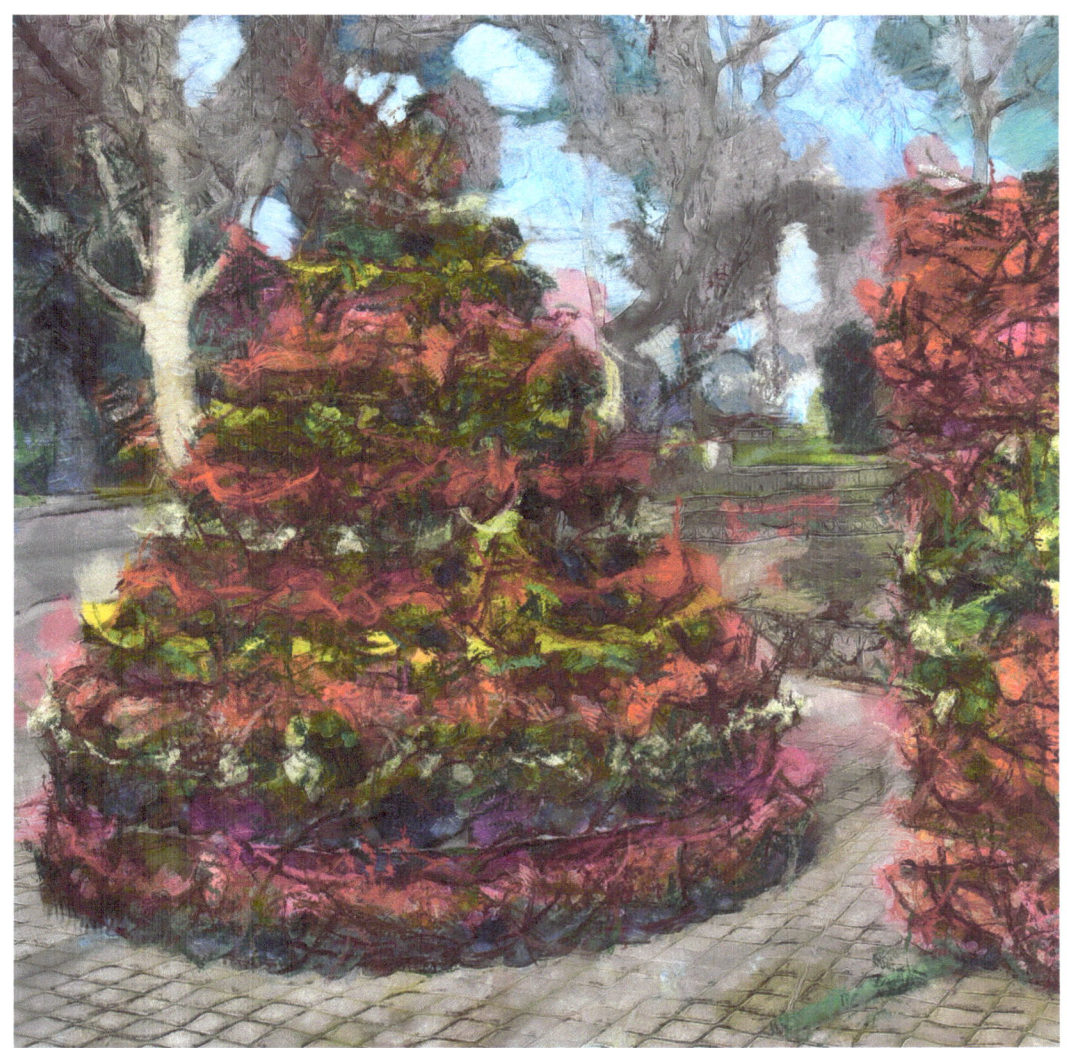

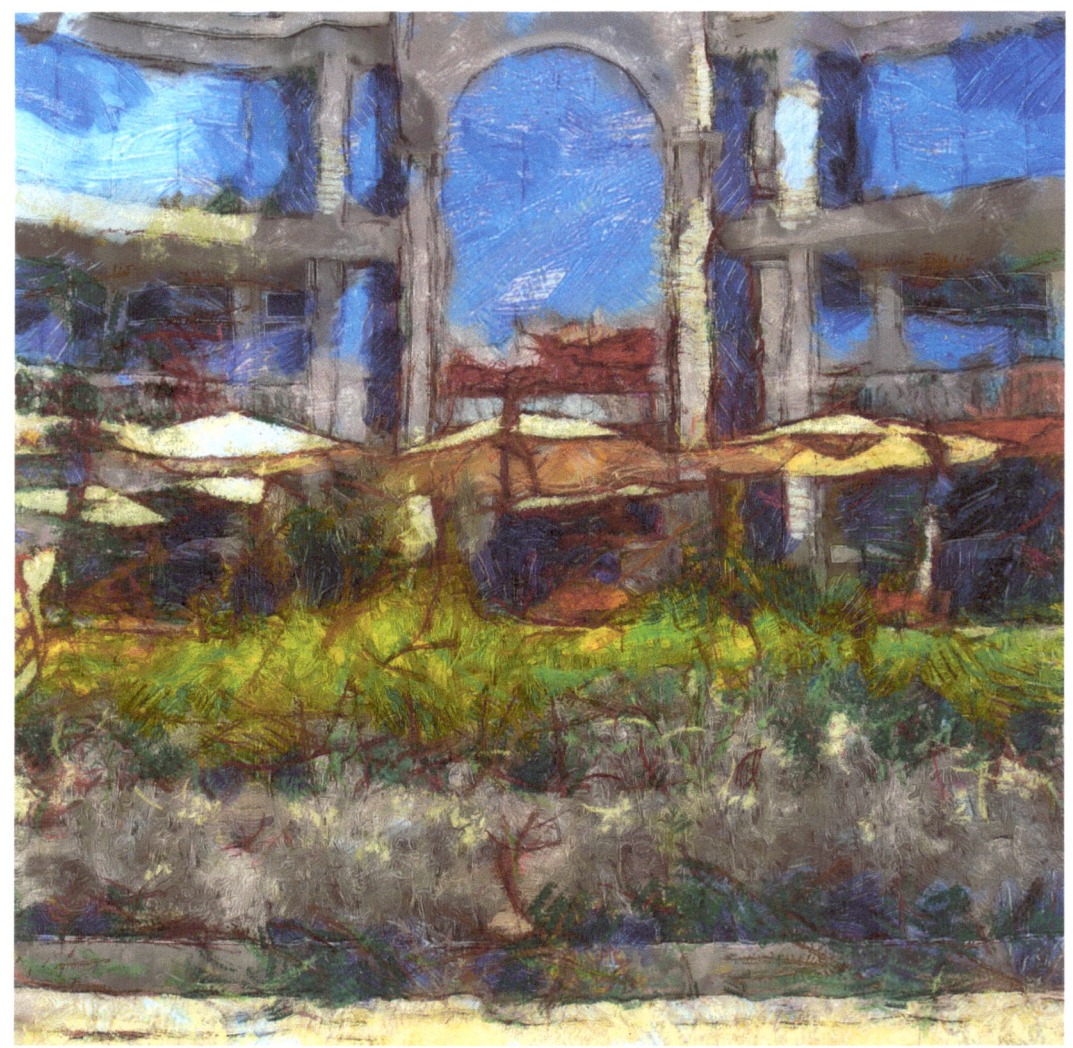

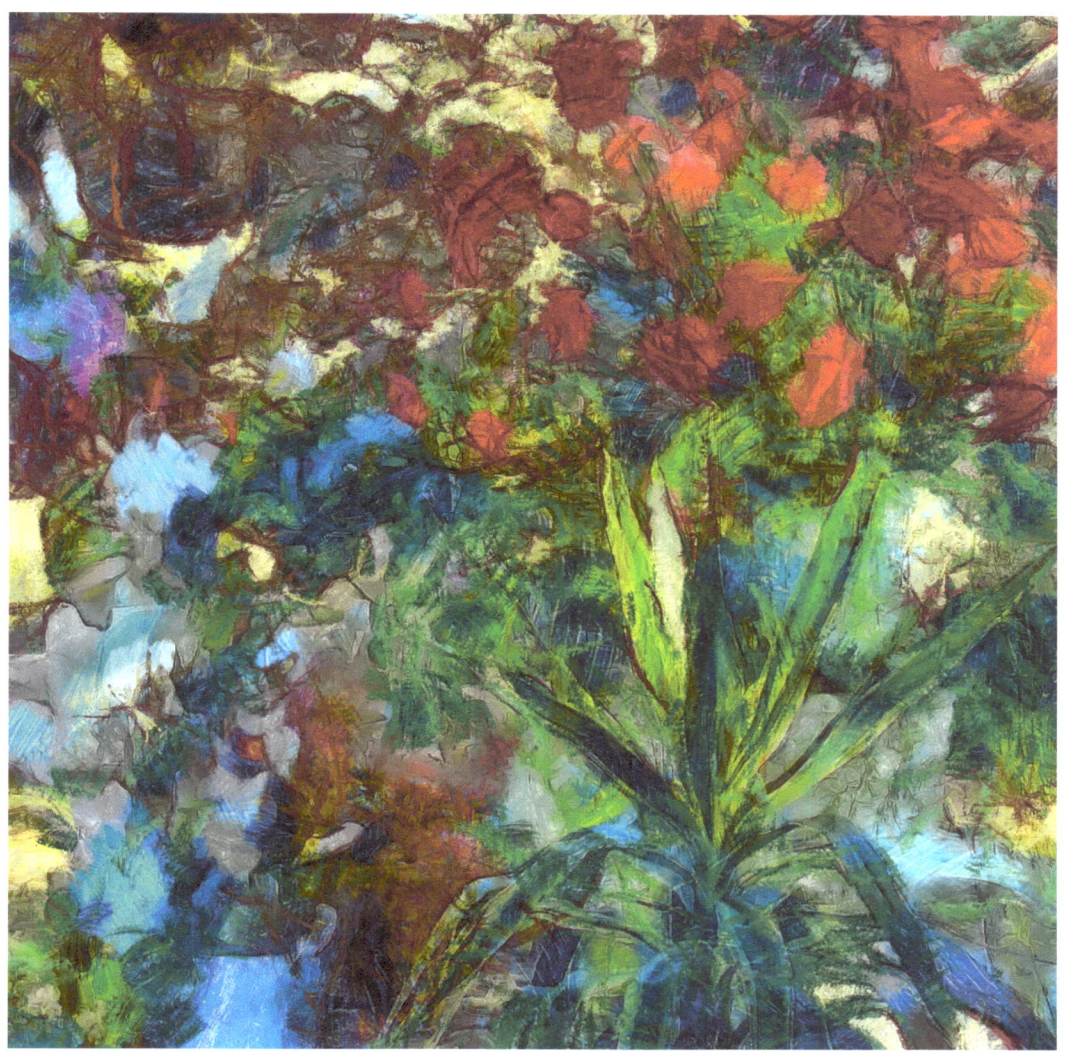

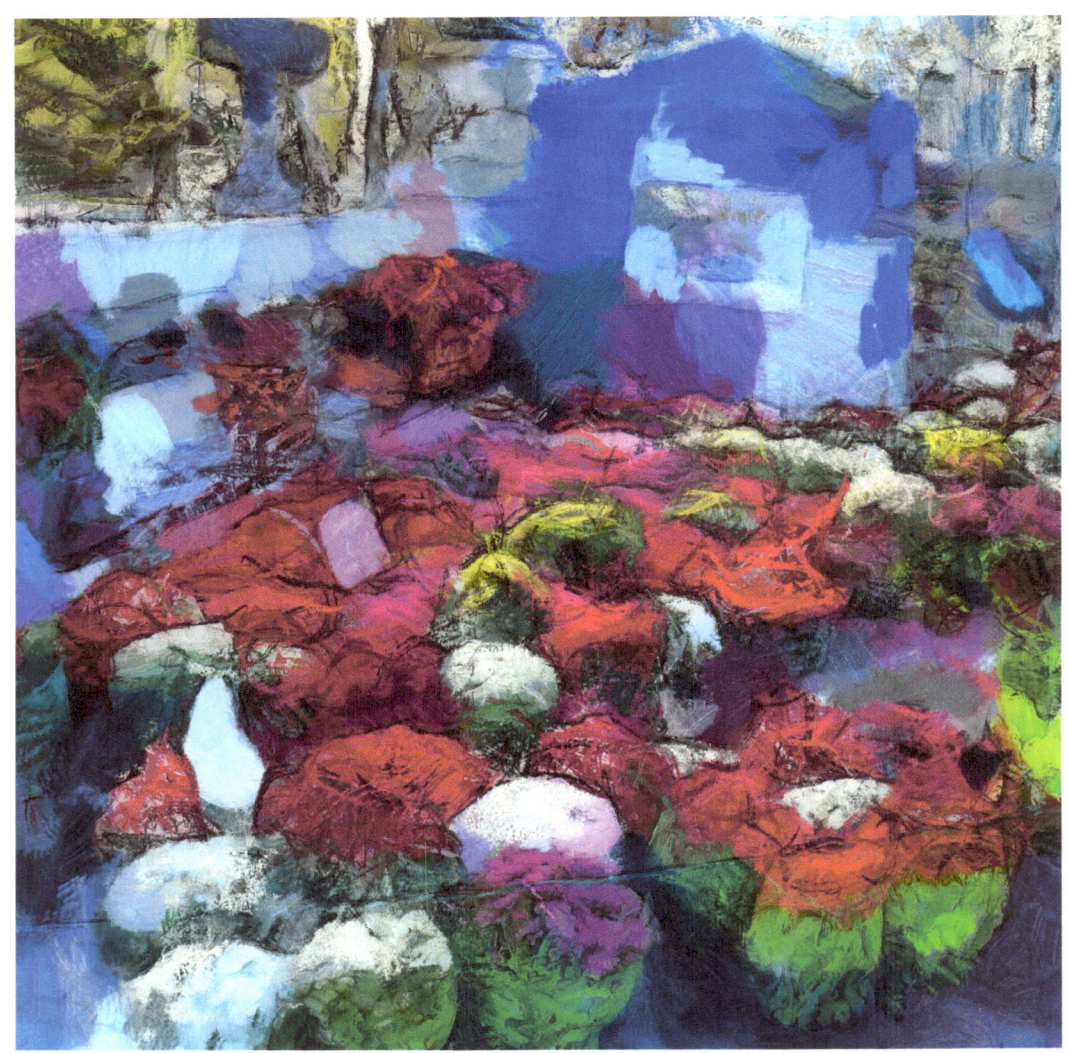

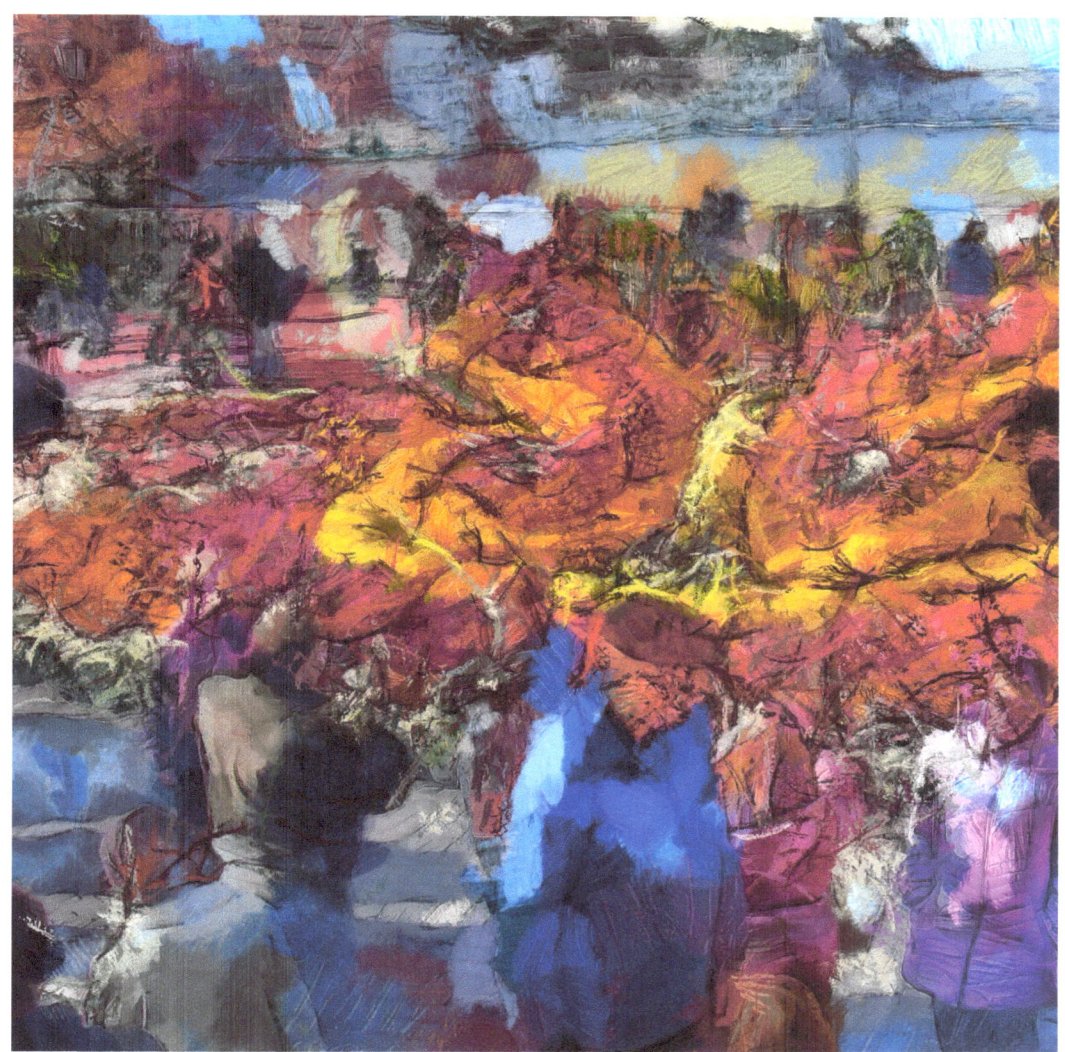

Alexander Cloudoncolorsky

.

ABOUT THE AUTHOR

List books of Cloudoncolorsky

#6 - Paul Gauguin … !
#5 - 21 century - Pupil of Vincent van Gogh
#4 - Painting of 21 century. Luminous Tulips.

#3 - The Painting Impressions for Children and Adult. 21 century.
www.createspace.com/5376721

#2 - The Painting Plus The Wise Quotes. 21 century.
www.createspace.com/5445703

#1 - Abstract Painting for Children and Adult. 21 century.
www.createspace.com/5276573

===-
If you have any questions for me, feel free to ask to an e-mail address:

alexandercorinthianis1.13@gmail.com

I will look forward to hearing from you.